THE MAKING OF

BLACK DOVES

A Fan's Unofficial Guide Through Season 1 of
the Spy Thriller: Unravel the Mysteries,
Analyze the Characters, and Explore the
Potential Future of the Series

MICHAEL S. SAGE

The Making of Black Doves

A Fan's Unofficial Guide Through
Season 1 of the Spy Thriller:
Unravel the Mysteries, Analyze
the Characters, and and Explore
the Potential Future of the Series

By

Michael S. Sage

Copyright© Michael S. Sage,2024

<u>Disclaimer</u>

All opinions, analyses, and interpretations expressed in this book are solely those of the author. While every effort has been made to ensure the accuracy of the information provided, this book is not intended to serve as an official source or substitute for the original series.

The use of character names, plot details, and other elements related to *Black Doves* is intended solely for editorial and informational purposes under the principles of fair use. All copyrights and trademarks remain the property of their respective owners.

<u>Limitation of Liability</u>

The information and content provided in this book are for informational and entertainment purposes only. While the author has made every effort to ensure the accuracy of the information at the time of writing, no representations or warranties, either express or implied, are made regarding the completeness, accuracy, reliability, or suitability of the content for any particular purpose. The author and publisher disclaim all liability for any errors, omissions, or inaccuracies in the content, or for any actions taken by readers based on the material provided in this book. By reading this book, you agree that the author and publisher will not be held responsible or liable for any loss, damage, or inconvenience, whether direct or indirect, resulting from the use or reliance on this publication.

This book is an independent and unauthorised work, and its content is not endorsed by or affiliated with any official parties involved in the creation or production of *Black Doves*. All rights to the series, characters, and related elements remain the property of their respective copyright holders. Readers are encouraged to watch the original series for the most accurate and official portrayal of the story and characters.

Gratitude

This book is a labour of love, inspired by the captivating world of *Black Doves* and the incredible artistry of those who brought the series to life. I extend my deepest gratitude to the creators, cast, crew, and everyone involved in crafting such a compelling story that sparked my imagination and compelled me to dive deeper into its intricacies.

To my readers, thank you for sharing this journey with me. Your enthusiasm for stories that challenge, inspire, and entertain is what fuels projects like this. I hope this book enhances your appreciation of *Black Doves* and provides new perspectives to enjoy.

Finally, to the fans of *Black Doves*—this book is for you. May it celebrate the series we love and inspire more conversations, theories, and shared excitement for what's to come. Thank you for being part of this community.

Table Of Contents

INTRODUCTION..9

    Why "Black Doves" Captures Our Imagination................9

    British Spy Thrillers' Legacy...12

Chapter 1: The Creation of Black Doves...........................17

    The Idea of Joe Barton: Creating a Modern Spy Thriller.17

    Behind the Scenes: Sister and Noisy Bear in the Production...20

    From Idea to Netflix: Securing the Deal.......................23

Chapter 2: Shooting the Mystery......................................25

    Lights, Camera, Action: Filming in London....................25

    Obstacles and Triumphs in Production..........................27

    The City's Role: London as a Persona...........................30

Chapter 3: Unpacking the Narrative..................................33

    A summary of the main points Danger, Betrayal, and Passion...33

    Analyzing the Spy Thriller Genre in Black Doves...........36

Chapter 4: The Characters of Black Doves.......................41

    Keira Knightley's "Helen": The Mysterious Lead............41

    Sarah Lancashire's "Reed": Enemy or Friend?..............43

    Ben Whishaw's "Sam": The Intriguing Ally.....................45

    Additional Important Figures: Jason, Alex, and the Ensemble Cast..47

Chapter 5: Motifs & Themes...51

    Loyalty and Secrets..51

    Love in the Shadows of Espionage...............................53

    Exploring Vulnerability and Power Dynamics.................55

Chapter 6: Speculations and Fan Theories......................59

    Who Can Be Trusted?...59

    Season 1's Unsolved Mysteries....................................63

Theories Regarding Helen's Hidden History................... 66
Chapter 7: Highlights of Season 1.................................... **69**
Ranking of the Best Episodes... 69
Important Moments and Cliffhangers............................ 72
Chapter 8: Reception and Cultural Impact...................... **77**
Early Buzz: Reviews and Fan Reactions to the Series... 77
The Role of Black Doves in Modern Streaming.............. 80
Chapter 9: Behind the Scenes... **85**
Insights from Interviews with the Cast and Crew........... 85
Easter Eggs and Secret Details...................................... 89
Chapter 10: The Hopes for Season 2 and Renewal.......... **93**
The Disclosure: Netflix's Belief in Black Doves.............. 93
Potential Storylines for Season Two............................. 95
What Fans Hope to See Up Next...................................98
CONCLUSION..**101**
The Black Dove's Allure.. 101
Future Plans for the Series and Its Fans......................102

INTRODUCTION

Why "Black Doves" Captures Our Imagination

Ever since Netflix made the announcement of Black Doves, it has captivated viewers worldwide. This British spy thriller promises to be an engrossing examination of love, treachery, and survival thanks to its intriguing premise, stellar cast, and Joe Barton's creative creativity. There is a tangible sense of mystery around Black Doves, which is fostered by the show's intriguing premise and the anticipation of its early second season renewal.

Fundamentally, Black Doves feeds on the contrasts between trust and betrayal, love and obligation, and secret and exposure. These components strike a chord with viewers because they reflect the intricacies of everyday life, albeit magnified in the high-stakes realm of espionage. Helen, portrayed by the unique Keira Knightley, is a prime example of these inconsistencies. Her intense relationship is more than simply a love side story; it's a risky entanglement that jeopardises her secret life. Our fascination with characters who traverse morally difficult situations, where every choice is a risk with potentially disastrous outcomes, is tapped into by this multi-layered narrative.

The setting of Black Doves is another aspect of its attractiveness. The intricate web of secrets and shadows that is London's underbelly makes the ideal setting for an espionage story. Brimming with historical intrigue and contemporary instability, the city serves as more than just a setting; it is a character unto itself, influencing the plot and its characters. Viewers are encouraged to investigate this dynamic setting, where peril lurks around every corner, through Helen's adventure.

Furthermore, Black Doves is unique in that it blends the high stakes of the spy genre with personal character drama. The suspense is there in both whispered talks and stolen moments, not just in action-packed scenes. The characteristic of a series that is expected to be as emotionally impactful as it is exciting is this combination of personal vulnerability and professional hazard.

Black Doves' outstanding ensemble cast is also largely responsible for the pre-release excitement surrounding the film. With Andrew Koji, Ben Whishaw, Sarah Lancashire, and Keira Knightley at the forefront, each actor gives their parts complexity and nuance, which helps the characters come across as real and approachable. Anticipation for the series is increased by these well-known performers who make sure the emotional weight and thrilling turns of the story are delivered with maximum force.

Last but not least, Netflix's early decision to renew Black Doves for a second season before the show's debut demonstrates their faith in the series' potential. This audacious approach shows that Black Doves is a series that is ready to make an impact on viewers and not merely a passing experiment. Black Doves is a drama that captivates our attention and won't let go because of its complex narrative weave and promise of durability.

British Spy Thrillers' Legacy

Black Doves continues the illustrious legacy of British spy thrillers, which have enthralled viewers for many years. Stories that explore the murky realm of espionage have long flourished in Britain, from John le Carré's complex Cold War tales to James Bond's thrilling adventures.

The emphasis on psychological depth is one of the characteristics that distinguish British spy thrillers. British stories typically examine the ethical dilemmas and personal costs of espionage, in contrast to their

American counterparts, which frequently place more emphasis on explosive action. Black Doves carries on this tradition by exploring the inner turmoil of Helen, the main character, as she juggles her desires with her secret identity. In addition to giving the story more depth, this contemplation forces spectators to think about the human cost of leading a secretive existence.

Another factor contributing to the genre's ongoing appeal is its realistic foundation. British spy thrillers are timeless and relevant because they frequently take cues from actual occurrences. Shows like Killing Eve and The Night Manager have demonstrated how contemporary espionage stories may be interwoven with current events, ranging from cyberwarfare to international politics. In a similar vein, Black Doves aims to ground its story in the grim reality of London's criminal underground, making it pertinent and approachable for viewers of today.

The capacity of British spy thrillers to combine suspense and intellect is another distinguishing feature. Classics like Tinker Tailor Soldier Spy, which combine complex narrative with gripping character studies, demonstrate this equilibrium. With a plot that alternates between intense action and private moments of tenderness, Black Doves seems ready to do the same. The series delivers more than simply cloak-and-dagger intrigue because of its emphasis on relationships, whether it is through the intense affair at its core or the bond between Helen and her mysterious protector Reed.

Another area in which British spy thrillers have changed recently is the inclusion of strong, complex female characters, and Black Doves is no exception. Helen, played by Keira Knightley, is more than just a helpless damsel; she is a multifaceted character whose decisions advance the plot. In a similar vein, Sarah Lancashire's Reed subverts gender norms in the genre by hinting at a heroine with her own secrets and goals.

It's also important to consider the aesthetic and ambiance that characterise British spy thrillers. These stories, which frequently feature rain-soaked streets and lavish drawing rooms, frequently contrast moments of luxury with stark realism. A similarly stirring backdrop will be provided by Black Doves' London location, which combines current gritty elements with historic beauty. The series gains further realism from the city's rich cinematic past, which fits in well with the espionage world's murky milieu.

Intentionally Left Blank

Chapter 1: The Creation of Black Doves

The Idea of Joe Barton: Creating a Modern Spy Thriller

Joe Barton, a gifted British producer and screenwriter who has made a name for himself in the field of high-concept, emotionally charged narrative, is at the centre of Black Doves. Barton is praised for his ability to combine complex character dynamics with genre clichés, and he is well-known for his work on critically acclaimed films like Giri/Haji and The Lazarus Project. Barton set out to write a spy thriller with Black Doves that explores the human condition in great detail while simultaneously captivating readers with its mystery and tension.

Barton's aim to investigate the intricacies of devotion and identity served as the foundation for his approach to Black Doves. Keira Knightley portrays the mysterious lead character Helen, who is caught between duty and desire. The plot revolves around her passionate affair, which sets off a chain of circumstances that forces her to face the delicate balance between her personal and professional responsibilities. This storyline gave Barton the chance to develop a protagonist character whose weaknesses made her all the more interesting and to question the conventional stereotypes frequently seen in espionage thrillers.

Barton's ability to firmly establish emotional realism in fantastical situations is a defining characteristic of his storytelling. He accomplishes this in Black Doves by emphasising the connections that propel the story. There are layers of tension, history, and hidden facts in the relationship between Helen and her old friend Reed (played by Sarah Lancashire), who is dispatched to protect her. In a similar vein, Helen's relationship with her doomed boyfriend gives an espionage-heavy plot a raw, emotional component.

Barton was also eager to update the espionage thriller genre, which has historically been dominated by stories that focus on men, when he wrote Black Doves. Barton aimed to subvert stereotypes of power and vulnerability by focussing the plot on a female protagonist, Helen, whose complexity defies simple classification. Her acts are motivated by a combination of personal and professional factors that are incredibly sympathetic, rather than being entirely heroic or wicked.

Barton's concept encompassed not only the characters but also the universe in which they live. With its unique combination of modern chaos and historic elegance, London is more than just a setting; it is a living, breathing part of the narrative. Reflecting the dualities at the core of Helen's quest, the city's winding alleyways and bustling underbelly make the ideal setting for a story of treachery and secrecy.

Behind the Scenes: Sister and Noisy Bear in the Production

Barton worked with Sister and Noisy Bear to realise his idea for Black Doves, which was a shared endeavour. Sister contributed a plethora of resources and experience to the production, having worked on highly acclaimed television shows including Chernobyl and This Is Going to Hurt. The production business was the perfect partner for Barton's ambitious concept because of its reputation for encouraging daring, creative storytelling.

The series' artistic design was greatly influenced by Barton's own production firm, Noisy Bear. Noisy Bear played a crucial role in making sure Black Doves stayed loyal to its creator's vision by emphasising the delivery of excellent, character-driven storytelling. Because he was both a writer and a producer, Barton was able to keep his vision consistent from the first script versions to the final edit.

The main location for filming was London, and production started in October 2023. The production crew purposefully chose to film on location in the city in order to convey the story's genuine vibe. The city's many environments, from the busy West End streets to the dim passageways of East London, added a visual depth that improved the story.

Under the direction of Keira Knightley, the ensemble contributed their own skills and originality. Knightley, who has acted in both contemporary blockbusters and historical dramas, accepted the challenge of capturing Helen's complex personality. The main cast was completed by Sarah Lancashire, Ben Whishaw, and Andrew Koji, all of whom gave performances that gave their roles more nuance and complexity.

The production crew had to deal with the typical difficulties of filming a high-stakes drama in a busy city. Careful preparation and execution were needed to capture the subtleties of the performances, keep narrative continuity, and coordinate complex action scenes. However, the team's commitment to excellence made sure that every obstacle was overcome with creativity and tenacity.

Beyond the practical aspects of production, Sister and Noisy Bear worked together to develop the series' artistic features. They collaborated to create a visual aesthetic that reflected the story's themes. For instance, the dualities of Helen's world were reflected through the use of light and shadow, while subtle colour shifts indicated variations in tension and tone. Despite their seeming insignificance, these nuances enhanced Black Doves' immersive experience by engrossing viewers in its complex web of mystery.

From Idea to Netflix: Securing the Deal

Black Doves was not an exception to the rule that the process from concept to screen is rarely simple. Nonetheless, the idea had a solid foundation thanks to Sister and Noisy Bear's support and Barton's reputation as a talented storyteller. Netflix, which is renowned for its dedication to creative and diverse programming, saw Black Doves' promise early on and acquired the distribution rights.

The collaboration with Netflix made it possible for Black Doves to reach a worldwide audience, guaranteeing that its themes of survival, love, and treachery would strike a chord with viewers well beyond its British roots. The series had the platform it required to thrive thanks to the streaming behemoth's resources and marketing clout, and its confidence in the project was demonstrated by the choice to renew it for a second season before its debut.

Additionally, landing the Netflix deal allowed Barton and his team to explore new creative possibilities. Because the streaming service was ready to take chances with unusual storylines, Barton was able to explore the story's darker and more nuanced elements without worrying about the story's integrity being compromised. In order to make Black Doves into the complex, emotionally complex thriller that it was meant to be, this creative freedom was essential.

Chapter 2: Shooting the Mystery

Lights, Camera, Action: Filming in London

In the middle of London's colourful and diverse metropolis, the production of Black Doves brought the dark world of espionage to life. The capital was the main venue for the filming, which started in October 2023. Its diverse array of attractions made for the ideal setting for a story full of romance, peril, and mystery.

The streets of London are teeming with contrasts: grandeur meets gritty, old history meets cutting-edge innovation. This contrast reflects Black Doves' themes, in which characters manage their own dualities by striking a balance between their personal and professional commitments. The city was more than just a setting for the production team; it was a silent participant in the drama that was developing.

A range of London locations were used to film key scenes, each selected to enhance the tone and plot of the series. The city offered Helen's story a constantly changing backdrop, from the vibrant bustle of Covent Garden to the dim passageways along the Thames. The capital's diversity and adaptability were demonstrated by the juxtaposition of lesser-known areas and secret passageways with iconic icons like the Shard and Tower Bridge.

Soundstages could never match the authenticity that came from filming on location. The series' suspense and emotional effect were increased by the texture and atmosphere that the real-world setting brought. For example, a crucial sequence in which Helen confronts an ally who turns against her was filmed at night on the soggy cobblestones of Soho, with the drama heightened by the dull glow of streetlights.

Additionally, some of London's more obscure and frightening locales were used in the production. The secret character of the plot was further reinforced by the utilisation of abandoned theatres, subterranean tunnels, and abandoned warehouses as crucial locations. The cast and crew were fully immersed in the world of Black Doves thanks to these areas, which were mainly unaffected by contemporary development and offered a sense of danger and timelessness.

Obstacles and Triumphs in Production

There were particular difficulties in filming in a city as energetic and lively as London. The city's enormous size and continuous activity necessitated careful preparation and organisation. The production team had to be quick-thinking to ensure a smooth shoot, from obtaining permissions for well-known locales to handling erratic weather.

Filming in public places was one of the biggest obstacles. London's busy streets are rarely deserted, and it frequently takes many hours of preparation to capture a dramatic moment in a crowded setting. The crew worked through the night, using deft camera angles and lighting methods to create an intimate ambiance despite the endless buzz of the city for situations that needed the illusion of solitude, like Helen's late-night rendezvous in a quiet park.

Another constant wild card in British cinema, the weather, proved to be both a help and a hindrance. Although unexpected downpours caused delays, they also gave some scenes a more dramatic feel. An unexpected shower served as the backdrop for a pivotal scene in which Helen considers her turbulent decisions. Despite being unplanned, the rain gave the scenario a moving visual metaphor that represented her inner agony.

Moreover, traffic created logistical challenges. It took effort and accuracy to plan vehicle chases and action scenes in London's winding streets. In one particularly striking scene, Helen speeds through the winding alleys of East London to elude a pursuer. Even though it looked amazing on television, weeks of preparation went into this exciting scene, which included several safety precautions, traffic diversion, and stunt choreography.

Notwithstanding these obstacles, the victories greatly exceeded the challenges. Because of the actors and crew's commitment, every challenge was turned into a creative opportunity. Always the epitome of professionalism, Keira Knightley handled the erratic situations with poise and produced amazing performances notwithstanding.

The greatest success of the production was its ability to create a complex narrative landscape in London. The city's well-known and obscure areas came to life, mirroring the changing moods of the narrative. Black Doves was a profoundly engaging experience that went beyond the usual spy thriller because of the harmonious fusion of the urban setting and the series' thematic components.

The City's Role: London as a Persona

London is much more than just a setting in Black Doves; it is a character unto itself. The plot and its characters are significantly shaped by the city's winding streets, old buildings, and evocative atmospheres. For Helen, London serves as both a haven and a battlefield, a place where truths are exposed and secrets are buried.

The show capitalises on the natural drama of the city. With its glass towers and Gothic spires, London's skyline illustrates how the past and present collide. The duality of Helen's life—caught between her secret life and her own passions—is reflected in this contrast. While scenes set in busy markets or pleasant cafes convey the warmth and unpredictable nature of her daily life, those set in tall office buildings reflect the cold, calculated world of espionage.

The story revolves around London's underground in particular. A realistic and menacing element is added by Barton's portrayal of the city's crime networks. Some of the most important scenes in the series take place in shadowy alleys, covert clubs, and abandoned warehouses, which represent the perils Helen must face. Although ominous, these settings also accentuate the characters' resourcefulness as they navigate dangerous areas.

However, London is more than just a dangerous city. It also provides beautiful and consoling moments. On Primrose Hill, beneath the glittering lights of the city, a touching conversation between Helen and her lover takes place. The momentary calm amid the turmoil of their lives is captured in this tableau, which is illuminated by the gentle glow of evening.

The series is also able to examine many aspects of London's identity because of the variety of the city's settings. Mirroring the inequalities in Helen's world, the wealthy neighbourhoods of Chelsea and Kensington stand in stark contrast to the industrial outskirts of Hackney and Shoreditch. The series' use of colour and lighting, which change to suit the atmosphere of each place, emphasises these differences even more.

In the end, London's role in Black Doves is just as nuanced and multi-layered as the people who live there. The story's themes permeate its streets, buildings, and secret nooks, creating a vibrant and always changing canvas. The city grows to represent Helen's personality as her voyage progresses, reflecting her setbacks, victories, and secrets.

Chapter 3: Unpacking the Narrative

A summary of the main points Danger, Betrayal, and Passion

A timeless and captivating story of desire, treachery, and peril is at the core of Black Doves. Keira Knightley plays Helen, a lady who leads a dualistic existence at the beginning of the series. Her calm façade belies a hidden identity connected to a mysterious organisation. When she has a passionate romance that sets off a chain of events that plunges her into the perilous underworld of London, her entire world starts to fall apart.

Helen's affair marks a significant turning point in the story and is more than just a romantic subplot. Her partner, who becomes embroiled in the criminal underbelly of London, becomes a liability as well as a source of emotional vulnerability.

The human aspect of Helen is exposed by this relationship; she is a woman whose decisions are influenced by love, guilt, and the need for connection. However, it also puts her in direct opposition to her work responsibilities, which creates the conditions for heartache and treachery.

Things get even more complicated when Reed (Sarah Lancashire), an old acquaintance sent by Helen's bosses to keep her safe, shows up. Reed's entrance creates a tense relationship that calls into question trust and commitment. The show's main themes are emphasised by the sense of mystery created by their shared past, which is alluded to but never fully disclosed. Does Reed have a personal goal, or is she there to protect Helen? This ambiguity, which reflects the show's dedication to complex, surprising narrative, keeps viewers guessing.

Helen must face the repercussions of her decisions as she negotiates the dangerous nexus of her personal and professional lives. London's criminal underworld is harsh, and alliances are both ephemeral and dangerous. Danger lurks around every corner, and friends turn into enemies. Helen's path is one of perseverance, survival, and navigating her moral limits on a continual basis.

The intensity of the story is reflected in the show's speed. Quieter, more contemplative moments that explore Helen's mind are intercut with high-stakes action sequences, including chases through the winding alleys of London or suspenseful encounters in dark warehouses. These changes produce a cadence that prevents viewers from becoming complacent and keeps them on edge.

The stakes have increased to an almost intolerable level by the end of the season. Helen's life is about to fall apart, and her future will be determined by the decisions she makes. Viewers are left with unanswered questions and the enticing prospect of additional surprises in later seasons.

Analyzing the Spy Thriller Genre in Black Doves

Although Black Doves is firmly anchored in the spy thriller genre's roots, it also aims to reinterpret its rules. The genre's core themes of deceit, secrecy, and high-stakes conflict are all present in Black Doves, which also adds a novel, character-driven viewpoint.

Historically, stoic, frequently masculine heroes who move with calculating precision through worlds of intrigue have dominated spy thrillers. But the focus of Black Doves is Helen, a multifaceted, emotionally complex female protagonist whose weakness is just as essential to her persona as her power. This change permits a more thorough examination of subjects like love, loyalty, and the personal costs of leading two lives, in addition to challenging the genre's gender conventions.

For example, Helen's affair is a narrative technique that gives the plot emotional depth in contrast to the usually clinical, cold relationships that are frequently shown in spy thrillers. Since Helen's personal decisions have a direct impact on her work life, this romance subplot heightens the tension that is already there in the genre rather than lessening it. Her dual life as a spy and a lover, a protector and a traitor, is representative of the show's larger examination of morality and identity.

A modernisation of the genre is also evident in Black Doves' narrative framework. Barton uses a more fragmented storytelling technique, disclosing important elements through flashbacks and broken dialogue, in contrast to the straight storytelling that was common in classic spy thrillers. This method not only deepens the mystery but also reflects Helen's own shattered identity.

Black Doves is firmly rooted in the spy thriller genre because of its portrayal of London as the backdrop. A story of intrigue and deceit would naturally take place against the backdrop of the city's winding streets, secret passageways, and constant observation. However, London is depicted with a uniqueness and richness that makes it more than just a scene. It takes on a life of its own, with rhythms and moods that mirror the complexities of the story.

In addition, Black Doves incorporates the genre's signature action scenes while keeping them realistic. The emphasis is still on their emotional stakes, even though there are high-octane moments of excitement, such chase chases and meticulously planned fight scenes. Because of the relationships and secrets involved, in addition to the physical danger, every confrontation is fraught with anxiety.

Black Doves' focus on moral ambiguity is another way it innovates in the spy thriller genre. Helen is a severely flawed heroine whose decisions are neither entirely right nor bad, in contrast to traditional narrative where heroes are clearly defined. The supporting cast is equally complex, with characters like Reed and Helen's enigmatic bosses functioning in morally dubious situations. A modern mentality that recognises the complexity of contemporary geopolitics and interpersonal relationships is reflected in this inability to make a clear distinction between good and evil.

Additionally, the series explores a topic that is frequently overlooked in the genre: the psychological costs of espionage. Unwavering honesty is used to portray Helen's ongoing watchfulness, her battle to uphold her dual identities, and the emotional toll of her choices. Because of its emphasis on the human cost of spying, Black Doves is both an exciting and incredibly sympathetic film.

Lastly, while establishing its own identity, Black Doves places itself within the larger tradition of British spy thrillers, taking cues from such masterpieces as *Tinker Tailor Soldier Spy* and *The Spy Who Came in from the Cold*. It is a deserving heir to these classic pieces because of its respect for the genre's heritage and its contemporary sensibility.

Chapter 4: The Characters of Black Doves

Keira Knightley's "Helen": The Mysterious Lead

Helen, a heroine of remarkable complexity and intrigue portrayed by Keira Knightley, is at the centre of Black Doves. Helen is a lady of action and vulnerability, a capable operative and a terribly damaged person, embodying the dualities that characterise the espionage thriller genre.

From the start, it is clear that Helen is mysterious. She leads a double life, keeping up an appearance of normalcy while hiding a hidden identity connected to an unidentified, mysterious organisation. Her character revolves around this deceit, and Knightley's subtle portrayal effectively conveys the conflict between Helen's personal aspirations and her work obligations.

A pivotal moment in the story occurs when Helen decides to have a passionate affair. Unknowingly, her lover sets off a chain of events that could endanger her life. Helen's fragility is shown by this relationship, revealing a side of her that is rarely seen in conventional espionage heroes. She is human, motivated by love, fear, and guilt; she is neither unbeatable nor dispassionate.

Knightley is a master of subtlety in her portrayal of Helen. She portrays the character's internal conflict—her attempt to balance her emotions with the perilous environment she lives in—through her facial expressions and body language. As captivating as the action scenes are Helen's reflective periods, in which she considers her decisions and their effects.

Helen's tenacity is revealed as the series goes on. She uses her knowledge and tenacity to navigate a dangerous and treacherous world, overcoming obstacles and outwitting her adversaries. However, there are costs associated with her voyage. Helen is one of the most complex and likeable characters in contemporary spy thrillers because of the difficult realities she must face as a result of her decisions.

Sarah Lancashire's "Reed": Enemy or Friend?

One of the most interesting characters in Black Doves is Reed, who is portrayed by the multifaceted Sarah Lancashire. Reed, who was sent by Helen's employers to keep her safe, adds a dynamic blend of uncertainty, conflict, and friendship.

Reed is positioned as a possible enemy as well as an ally. From the beginning, it is implied that she and Helen are connected, implying a shared past that makes their relationship more difficult. This ambiguity is conveyed in Lancashire's performance, which gives Reed a combination of warmth and coldness. Though her acts and reasons are yet unknown, she is extremely protective of Helen.

Reed's moral ambiguity is what makes her so captivating. Reed is more than just Helen's bodyguard or defender, as is customary in espionage stories. Because of her personal commitments and duties, she functions in a morally ambiguous environment. As a result, Helen and Reed have to carefully manage their relationship by striking a balance between mistrust and trust.

There is a sense of gravity to Lancashire's portrayal. With each measured and purposeful action, Reed radiates a quiet strength. She does, however, occasionally let her guard down, showing glimmers of emotion and vulnerability. These scenes allude to a closer bond with Helen and imply that Reed's role in the narrative is far more intimate than it first seems.

Viewers are kept wondering by Reed's mysterious personality whether she genuinely supports Helen or if she has ulterior motives. Reed is one of the series' most notable characters because of this ambiguity, which heightens the suspense.

Ben Whishaw's "Sam": The Intriguing Ally

Ben Whishaw's character Sam is difficult to put into one category. Sam is introduced as Helen's ally, yet his function in the story is just as nuanced as the guy himself.

Sam is not your typical agent or spy. As someone who lives on the periphery of Helen's world, he instead occupies a liminal place. He is a great asset because of his knowledge, ingenuity, and modest manner, but his relationship with Helen is what really makes him who he is.

Whishaw creates a figure who is both friendly and mysterious by giving Sam a subdued energy. Subtext abounds in his exchanges with Helen, implying a level of comprehension and bond that transcends simple companionship. Despite being one of Helen's few confidants, Sam and Helen have a tense relationship.

One important source of interest is Sam's motivations. Even if he seems to support Helen, there are times when his behaviour suggests a secret objective. Because of this ambiguity, he is a volatile character who, depending on the circumstance, can turn from an ally to an enemy.

Sam's moral compass is one of his distinguishing characteristics. Sam stands out as someone who considers the moral ramifications of his decisions in a society where morality is pliable and devotion is frequently conditional. His character is given depth by this internal conflict, which also makes him an intriguing contrast to Helen, whose pragmatism frequently causes her to make ethically dubious choices.

Additional Important Figures: Jason, Alex, and the Ensemble Cast

Each of Black Doves' supporting characters contributes complexity and relevance to the story, enhancing it. Among them, the ensemble cast, Jason, and Alex all have significant influences on Helen's path and the environment she lives in.

- *(Andrew Koji) Jason:* Jason is an enigmatic and dynamic character who hovers between an ally and an enemy. Jason, who is portrayed by Andrew Koji, gives the series a sense of danger with his energy and physicality. Tension permeates his contacts with Helen, suggesting an unacknowledged conflict or shared past. Jason plays a crucial part in the story since he is both a danger and a possible solution to Helen's survival.
- *Tracey Ullman's character Alex:* Tracey Ullman's portrayal of Alex gives the narrative depth and

complexity. Alex is an older, more seasoned character in Helen's world who acts as a mentor and a warning. Alex is a captivating presence because of Ullman's portrayal, which effectively conveys her wisdom and tiredness. She plays a number of roles in the narrative, serving as both Helen's mentor and a reminder of the costs associated with their profession.

- *The entire cast:* In addition to these main characters, Black Doves has a strong ensemble cast that deepens the story's complexities. Every character adds to the series' fabric, from Omari Douglas's astute confidant to Kathryn Hunter's mysterious agent. The world of Black Doves feels real and alive because these people are more than just supporting cast members; they each have their own goals, secrets, and storylines.

The series is filled with talented actors that can give complex performances, thanks to the casting of Adeel Akhtar, Ella Lily Hyland, and Gabrielle Creevy, among others. These actors give their roles depth and conviction, whether they are portraying antagonists, allies, or morally ambiguous characters.

The series is grounded in a reality that feels both particular and universal, thanks to the ensemble cast's diversity, which also represents London's international spirit. Every character's tale contributes to the depth of Black Doves, from the high-stakes machinations of criminal leaders to the more subdued hardships of those caught in the crossfire.

Intentionally Left Blank

Chapter 5: Motifs & Themes

Black Doves' depth and appeal come from its examination of issues and motifs that cut much beyond the usual boundaries of the spy thriller genre. The series explores common human experiences—secrets, love, power, and vulnerability—through its complex narrative and likeable characters, all the while placing them in the murky realm of espionage.

Loyalty and Secrets

The subject of concealment, which is characteristic of the spy thriller genre, is central to Black Doves. From Helen to her allies and enemies, each character must negotiate a society based on carefully guarded identities, covert objectives, and half-truths. For Helen, secrets are the cornerstone of her life, not just a necessary professional requirement. Her dual existence as a woman battling personal impulses and a proficient operative highlights the psychological toll of leading a life rife with deceit.

In Black Doves, secrecy is not shown as a simple strength or weakness. It is a two-edged sword instead. Helen's capacity to hide who she really is helps her live in a perilous world, but it also keeps her apart from important relationships. This tension is best illustrated by her affair with her boyfriend, which poses a threat to her well crafted façade. The show examines how, although protective, secrets may sometimes serve as obstacles that impede closeness and trust.

Another recurring motif is loyalty as a counterbalance to secrecy. The protagonists in Black Doves must negotiate changing sands of trust in a society where loyalty is frequently ephemeral and transactional. Helen's guardian, Reed, is a prime example of this uncertainty. Although her devotion to Helen appears sincere, it is unclear where her real loyalties lie given that she is an agent of Helen's employers.

Viewers are prompted by the series to reflect on the complexities of loyalty in a morally ambiguous environment. When devotion necessitates sacrificing one's morals, is it still a virtue? Is secrecy inherently incompatible with it, or can they coexist? Black Doves challenges us to consider these issues through its complex character interactions, elevating loyalty above a simple plot device to a serious ethical conundrum.

Love in the Shadows of Espionage

In Black Doves, the contrast between espionage and love is both heartbreaking and tense. A major theme that unites Helen's personal and professional facets of her life, her affair is more than just a romantic side story. In the series, love is presented as both a source of power and a possible weakness.

From the beginning, Helen's connection with her lover is dangerous. Emotional ties are liabilities in the secret society she lives in, yet Helen lets herself be sucked into a passionate relationship. This choice demonstrates her longing for normalcy and connection, which contrast sharply with the calculating, icy tone of her job.

Love is shown in the program as a force that has the capacity to both empower and threaten. On the one hand, Helen's relationship highlights her humanity and serves as a reminder to viewers that people want closeness and understanding even in the most dangerous situations. However, it is precisely this relationship that initiates a series of circumstances that jeopardises her well preserved confidentiality.

The relationship between Reed and Sam and Helen further muddies the love concept.

Their connections with her have a strong emotional resonance even though they are not explicitly romantic. Sam's devotion and Reed's protectiveness point to types of love that go beyond romance and include friendship, companionship, and possibly unsaid love.

Black Doves explores the risks and sacrifices associated with both espionage and love by examining their interconnections. In this situation, love is a battleground rather than a haven, where treachery and weakness are inevitable.

Exploring Vulnerability and Power Dynamics

Another important theme in Black Doves is the tension between vulnerability and power, which shapes the story and its characters. Power fluctuates between people and organisations in the murky realm of espionage. As the main character, Helen navigates a world where relationships and hierarchies are always shifting while simultaneously wielding and being victimised by power.

Helen is shown as a strong, capable woman because of her work as a spy. She works precisely, outwitting opponents and demonstrating incredible perseverance in times of crisis. Her personal hardships, however, show a sensitivity that stands in stark contrast to her professional image. The emotional toll that her existence has taken is emphasised by her affair, her dependence on Reed, and her reflective periods.

Reed's persona represents yet another aspect of power relations. She has some authority because she is Helen's guardian, but she is in a secondary role because of her devotion to her employers. She is a compelling character because of this duality, having to always strike a balance between her obligations and her personal beliefs. The ambiguities of power are further highlighted by Reed's encounters with Helen. Although she is entrusted with Helen's protection, their emotional past points to a more complex and nuanced relationship.

In Black Doves, the criminal underworld of London is portrayed as a microcosm reflecting broader power dynamics. The show depicts a society in which authority is negotiated rather than absolute, frequently through deceit, threats, and manipulation. Helen's interactions with members of this underworld highlight how unstable her position is. Despite her abilities, she is always in danger, and the personal stakes make her even more vulnerable.

In Black Doves, vulnerability is presented as an inherent aspect of the human condition rather than as a sign of weakness. The high-stakes drama is grounded in emotional reality by Helen's genuine and empathetic moments of uncertainty and anxiety. According to the series, real strength is found in navigating weakness rather than avoiding it.

Chapter 6: Speculations and Fan Theories

Fans' imaginations have been sparked by Black Doves since its announcement, leading to countless conversations regarding its characters, plot twists, and hidden meanings. As viewers try to connect together hints and predict the surprises that lie ahead, Joe Barton's multilayered world invites study and discussion. This chapter examines some of the most fascinating fan ideas and conjectures about the show, delving into issues of trust, unsolved mysteries, and Helen's mysterious past.

Who Can Be Trusted?

In the world of Black Doves, where relationships are shaky and motives are frequently unclear, trust is a rare commodity. The motives of almost every character have been quickly questioned by fans, and a number of theories have been put forth on which characters may actually be trusted.

Reed: Guardian or Puppet?

In conversations concerning trust, Sarah Lancashire's character Reed is arguably the most controversial. Reed, who was sent by Helen's employers to keep her safe, comes out as capable and devoted. Her loyalty to the company that hires Helen, however, raises questions about her actual intentions.

According to a widely accepted belief, Reed is entrusted with keeping an eye on Helen and making sure she complies, acting as both a watchdog and a protector. The conflict in their relationship and Reed's sporadic hesitancy to fully back Helen's choices may be explained by this dual position. According to a different viewpoint, Reed may have personal allegiances to Helen that clash with her work commitments, perhaps causing their relationship to change.

Sam: The Secret Plan?

Another character whose credibility is hotly contested is Sam, who is portrayed by Ben Whishaw. At first glance, Sam seems like a loyal friend who supports Helen during her difficult times. His mysterious manner and sporadic concealment, however, have prompted some admirers to hypothesise that he might be employed by an unidentified organisation, perhaps with goals at odds with Helen's.

According to a subset of hypotheses, Sam's seeming devotion to Helen is a component of a bigger plot. Does he have a covert connection to London's criminal underworld, or is he operating under duress? Sam is one of the most fascinating characters because of these possibilities, as his actual nature is still tantalisingly mysterious.

The Organisation: Friend or Enemy?

Despite spending most of Season 1 in the background, Helen's employers have a significant impact on the story. Supporters have conjectured that the organisation might not be what it seems to be. Is it possible that Helen is only a piece in a bigger puzzle, her abilities being used for reasons she doesn't completely comprehend?

According to some views, Helen's bosses may even be planning the threats she experiences, using her as a test subject or as bait in a bigger plot. If accurate, this information might be a turning point in the plot that forces Helen to face not just her adversaries but also those she thought were on her side.

Season 1's Unsolved Mysteries

By the end of its first season, Black Doves, like any compelling spy thriller, leaves viewers with a lot of unsolved concerns. Many theories have been proposed by fans in an effort to explain these unsolved mysteries.

Who Killed Helen's lover?

The death of Helen's lover, which starts a series of events that jeopardises her meticulously planned existence, is one of the main mysteries of Season 1. Although members of London's criminal underworld are among the apparent candidates, fans have suggested other murderers.

According to some theories, Helen's bosses may have planned the murder in order to control her or try her allegiance. Others speculate that the murderer may be a member of Helen's past with very personal motives. This question will continue throughout Season 2 since the real answer is still unclear.

What Is the Real Goal of the Organisation?

There is also interest in the mysterious company that hires Helen. Although its operatives seem to function with authority and accuracy, nothing is known about its ultimate objectives. The organisation may not be a conventional intelligence agency, but rather a private organisation with its own goals, according to fan speculation.

Is it possible that the organisation engages in illicit operations and uses its employees as unintentional enforcers? Or is it playing a bigger geopolitical game, influencing world events? As Helen must make her way through a world where even her employers might not be reliable, these questions heighten the suspense of her journey.

What Are the Motives of the Criminal Underworld?

Black Doves heavily relies on the London underground, which is both a source of intrigue and an antagonistic force. But it's still unclear exactly how it played a role in Helen's life.

Some fans think that Helen is being targeted by the underworld's leaders as part of a bigger grudge against her organisation rather than because of her individual deeds. Others speculate that Helen's affair might have unintentionally revealed private information, inciting the wrath of the underworld. These theories highlight how the plotlines and characters in the series are intertwined, weaving a complex web of intrigue and conflict.

Theories Regarding Helen's Hidden History

One of the most mysterious elements of Black Doves is Helen's backstory. Fans have been quick to speculate about the events that turned her into the skilled but troubled operative we see on film, even if Season 1 focusses on her current struggles.

A Horrible Start?

According to a widely accepted belief, Helen was forced or desperate into joining the organisation rather than voluntarily. Maybe a personal tragedy, like losing a loved one or being betrayed by someone she trusted, drew her into the world of espionage. Her cautious demeanour and her hesitancy to completely trust even her closest allies might be explained by this backstory.

A Double Life Right From the Beginning?

Helen has been leading a secret life for much longer than anyone understands, according to another theory. Before being hired by the organisation, fans have conjectured that she might have been a part of illegal activity or underground networks. Given that Helen's past may be as ambiguous as the world she currently lives in, this argument would be consistent with the show's themes of moral ambiguity.

A Personal Relationship with the Organisation?

According to several admirers, Helen has very intimate connections to the organisation. Could she be associated with its leadership, as a protégé or cousin of a senior officer? This relationship would account for the organization's strong interest in protecting her and the degree of liberty she is given, which appears out of character for someone in her role.

The part the lover played in her past

There is certainly room for conjecture regarding Helen's relationship with her partner. Did her partner have any connection to her background or her job, or was this a completely passionate relationship? Her partner may have been aware of her hidden identity, according to some fans' theories, which would have complicated their connection even more. If accurate, this information might have a big impact on Helen's path in later seasons.

Chapter 7: Highlights of Season 1

Black Doves' status as a premier spy thriller was cemented in Season 1 with its compelling fusion of suspense, mystery, and emotional depth. With its twists, discoveries, and memorable moments, each episode added to the overall plot and left viewers eagerly awaiting the next installment. In this chapter, we rate the season's top episodes and discuss the pivotal scenes and cliffhangers that shaped the series' premiere.

Ranking of the Best Episodes

Episode 6: "Beneath the Mask"

Suspense and emotional intensity are masterfully displayed in the season's penultimate episode. As her lover's secrets are revealed, Helen's meticulously preserved façade breaks down, exposing a deeper connection to London's criminal underground. A climactic showdown that sets the scene for the climax results from Reed's allegiance being tested to the limit.

This episode is notable for its relentless pacing and character-driven storyline. It is a highlight of the series because of the unexpected betrayal by a valued ally and the discoveries regarding Helen's history.

Episode 1: *"The Dove Takes Flight"*

The series' tone is established in the season opening, which skilfully and elegantly introduces Helen and her dual life. With a dramatic operation gone wrong and the start of her passionate but risky affair, the episode immediately immerses viewers in the high-stakes world of espionage.

The London setting provides an atmospheric touch to the developing story, and Keira Knightley's powerful performances as Helen and the supporting characters instantly captivate the audience.

Episode 8: "The Edge of the Abyss"

While certain plotlines are resolved in the season finale, others are left tantalisingly open. It offers a compelling mix of action and emotion. With her life and independence on the line, Helen battles her worst enemy to date.

Viewers are left reeling by the final moments, which include a heartbreaking betrayal and an unexpected reconciliation. Fans will be eager to return for Season 2 because of the episode's cliffhanger.

Episode 4: "Through the Looking Glass"

This midseason episode delves deeply into Helen's mind, examining her anxieties and motivations. She struggles with the consequences of her double existence in a rare moment of vulnerability. Sam discovers a crucial piece of information in the interim that raises the possibility of a wider conspiracy within the company.

This episode stands out due to its skilfully constructed suspense and emotionally driven performances.

Episode 3: "Shadows and Silhouettes"

This episode demonstrates how well the series combines complex character development with action. As they embark on a high-stakes mission together, Helen and Reed's relationship vacillates between friendship and suspicion. In order to add even more suspense to the story, the episode also presents a mysterious character from Helen's past.

Important Moments and Cliffhangers

There are several memorable moments in Black Doves' first season, each of which deepens the plot and gives the characters more nuance. Highlights include the following:

1. *The Death of Helen's Lover (Episode 2)*

The death of Helen's lover, the series' inciting incident, is both horrific and crucial. Because of the scene's intense emotional impact, Helen is forced to face the personal hazards associated with her career. The story begins at this point, weaving together Helen's personal grief with the more extensive schemes of the criminal underground.

2. *The Secret Plan of Reed (Episode 5)*

When it becomes apparent that Reed might be harbouring secrets of her own, her persona takes a darker turn. Fans are left wondering about her true allegiances as a mysterious phone call raises the possibility of a betrayal. Her relationship with Helen becomes more tense as a result of this revelation, which leads to an intensely emotional and stressful confrontation.

3. *The Power Play in the Underworld (Episode 6)*

When a secret rendezvous degenerates into a lethal ambush, the impact of the criminal underworld is made abundantly clear. Although Helen barely escapes, the incident makes clear how serious the threat she confronts is. This is a pivotal occasion that makes Helen reevaluate her plans and partnerships.

4. *Sam's Startling Discovery (Episode 7)*

In one of the most shocking turns of the season, Sam discovers proof that Helen's employers might have planned the murder of her lover. This discovery's ramifications reverberate throughout the story, challenging Helen's presumptions.

Sam's character is further developed by this revelation, which casts him as either a hesitant conspirator or a possible whistleblower.

5. *Helen's Betrayal: The Finale Cliffhanger (Episode 8)*

Helen suffers a crushing blow in the season's closing moments when she is betrayed by an unexpected person. She is left defenceless and alone as she faces an unclear future as a result of the betrayal, which is both emotional and professional.

In the eerie final scene of the episode, Helen is seen leaving the rubble of her life with a dejected yet determined expression. With more twists and secrets to come, the cliffhanger sets up Season 2 as Helen's reckoning.

Intentionally Left Blank

Chapter 8: Reception and Cultural Impact

Due to its ambitious plot, outstanding cast, and Joe Barton's reputation as a master storyteller, Black Doves' premiere was greeted with a great deal of excitement and conversation. From its initial teases to its debut, the series enthralled viewers and reviewers alike, establishing a distinct niche in the congested field of contemporary streaming. The cultural impact of Black Doves is examined in this chapter, along with its critical reception and positioning in relation to current streaming trends.

Early Buzz: Reviews and Fan Reactions to the Series

Black Doves created a lot of interest as soon as it was unveiled. The participation of Joe Barton, whose earlier works such as Giri/Haji received a great deal of praise, ensured a certain amount of interest among spy thriller enthusiasts. Excitement was further heightened by the addition of talents like Andrew Koji, Sarah Lancashire, and Ben Whishaw, as well as by the casting of Keira Knightley as the mysterious Helen.

Crucial Responses

Critics gave Black Doves mostly favourable reviews when it was first released. Its emotional depth and narrative intricacy were often cited as its most notable features. The show was commended by many for its ability to strike a balance between the political and the personal, tying Helen's emotional battles into more general issues of identity, power, and allegiance.

Widespread praise was also given to the performances. While Sarah Lancashire's Reed was frequently singled out as a scene-stealer, Knightley's portrayal of Helen was praised for being "nuanced and commanding." Critics praised the show's exploration of the characters' humanity rather than the flat depictions typical of spy thrillers.

The pacing, especially in the series' mid-season episodes, was pointed out by some critics as a possible problem. The slower scenes occasionally felt out of step with the high-stakes tension that the premise promised, even as they allowed for more in-depth character development. Others, however, defended this strategic pacing as a brave decision that deepened the psychological depth of the program.

Fan Reactions

Black Doves were quickly embraced by fans, and hypotheses and interpretations were rife on social media and online forums. Debates concerning motives, allegiances, and covert objectives were sparked by the show's ethically dubious characters and multi-layered storytelling, which compelled viewers to interact closely with the content.

The character of Helen was among the most talked-about elements. Regarding her choices, fans were split; some questioned her discernment, while others praised her fortitude. As viewers tried to analyse her decisions and forecast her future course of action, this polarity only increased interest in her path.

The London setting of the series also struck a deep chord with viewers, who valued how the city was portrayed as both a background and a distinct character. London's rough yet realistic depiction gave the story more realism and grounded its high-stakes espionage in a real-world setting.

The Role of Black Doves in Modern Streaming

Black Doves stands out in the crowded streaming market of today not only for its ambitious storyline but also for its calculated approach to fan interaction. Series like Black Doves show the value of ageless and contemporary narrative as streaming services compete for viewers' attention.

The Transition to Intricate Storylines

Today's streaming viewers are looking for stories that question, provoke, and resonate on several levels; they are no longer satisfied with mere amusement. This tendency is best shown by Black Doves, which provides a story that is both emotionally complex and gripping.

While placing them in the high-stakes realm of espionage, the series' examination of topics like identity, loyalty, and power dynamics draws on universal human experiences. With its blend of political and personal narrative, Black Doves joins other highly regarded streaming shows like Bodyguard and Killing Eve.

Furthermore, the show's reluctance to offer simple solutions fits well with viewers' increasing need for ethically nuanced stories. Black Doves challenges viewers to think on the subtleties of human behaviour and ethical quandaries by showcasing characters that are ambiguous.

Serving International Audiences

Since Black Doves is a Netflix production, its appeal cuts beyond cultural barriers and is intended for a worldwide audience. Despite having strong ties to its British heritage, the show's themes and characters are international and appeal to audiences all over the world.

The show's worldwide appeal is increased by the inclusion of well-known performers like Keira Knightley and Ben Whishaw, and its intricate portrayal of London provides a genuine yet approachable glimpse into British society. The show's success in the cutthroat streaming industry depends on striking a balance between local specificity and global significance.

Redefining the genre of spy thrillers

Black Doves reimagines what fans anticipate from an espionage thriller in a number of ways. The series prioritises character development and emotional depth over conventional genre cliches, even if there are action-packed scenes and high-stakes missions.

The blurring of genre boundaries in contemporary streaming is reflected in this strategy. Black Doves appeals to a wide range of viewers by fusing aspects of mystery, romance, and drama, including those who might not normally enjoy spy thrillers.

Traditional ideas of who gets to lead stories in this genre are also challenged by the series' emphasis on a female protagonist. Helen is more than simply a spy; she is a complicated person who struggles with identity, love, and grief. Her experience highlights the psychological and emotional costs of espionage and brings a new viewpoint to the genre.

The Function of Fandom and Social Media

In the era of streaming, a show's cultural impact is greatly influenced by fan interaction, and Black Doves has been no exception. A thriving online community has been sparked by the series, with fans discussing thoughts, writing analyses, and producing artwork on sites like Tumblr, Reddit, and Twitter.

This degree of involvement is indicative of a larger tendency in contemporary media consumption, when viewers actively take part in the narrative. Black Doves maintains its audience's interest in between episodes and seasons by promoting debate and conjecture, guaranteeing its position in the cultural discourse.

Chapter 9: Behind the Scenes

Like any great television show, Black Doves' success is due to the talent and commitment of its cast and staff as well as its compelling narrative. In addition to revealing the secret elements and Easter eggs weaved throughout the story, this chapter takes readers behind the scenes by giving insights from conversations with the people who made the program possible.

Insights from Interviews with the Cast and Crew

A team of gifted people worked together to bring Black Doves from script to screen, each bringing their specialisation to create an engaging spy thriller. Interviews with the cast and crew show how much planning and teamwork went into the production.

Keira Knightley on Her Helen Role

In interviews, Keira Knightley, who played the mysterious lead character Helen, discussed the intricacies of her role. *"She's not your normal spy,"* Knightley clarified. I was drawn to her because of her complexity, vulnerability, and genuine humanity. Her path, juggling the duties of espionage with her personal losses, has a rawness to it. It is a narrative that questions the notion of strength.

Knightley also talked about the role's physical requirements, like learning complex choreography for action scenes and performing stunts. It was exciting, but it also gave Helen a deeper level of realism. She is more sympathetic because she is resourceful and determined, not untouchable.

Sarah Lancashire on the Dual Nature of Reed

The actress who played Reed, Sarah Lancashire, called her role a study in paradoxes. Lancashire revealed, *"Reed is extremely guarded but fiercely loyal."* She works in the background, and it's precisely this uncertainty that draws people in. Is she an enemy or a friend? Reed herself doesn't always know what her loyalties are.

As part of his approach to the character, Lancashire explored Reed's motivations and past, most of which is only alluded to in the series. "I wanted to give her depth so that viewers could relate to her struggles and question her actions."

Joe Barton on Script Writing

Black Doves' author and creator, Joe Barton, stated that he was inspired by the idea of reinventing the spy thriller genre. Although I've always enjoyed spy fiction, I wanted to examine it from a more intimate perspective. What occurs when the distinction between personal and professional life becomes hazy? The core of Black Doves is found there.

Barton praised the cast and crew's contributions and underlined the project's collaborative aspect. From the filmmakers' vision to the actors' interpretations, each one contributed something special. It's what gave the series such a vibrant and lively feel.

The Crew Behind the Scenes

The production crew encountered a number of difficulties, especially when filming the intricate action scenes in the busy streets of London. Laura Bellingham, the cinematographer, emphasised the significance of depicting the dichotomy of the city. We aimed to capture the beauty and gritty side of London in each shot. Like the story's people, the city is full of secrets.

The garment selections, which delicately convey the personalities and storylines of the characters, were also discussed by costume designer Sinead Kidao. As the story goes on, Helen's outfit changes to reflect her journey. She appears polished and in control at first, but as her world falls apart, her appearance grows more vulnerable.

Easter Eggs and Secret Details

Throughout the series, the Black Doves creative team incorporated subtle allusions and hints, rewarding viewers who paid attention and giving the narrative more depth. Some of the most fascinating Easter eggs and secret information to be on the lookout for are as follows:

1. *The Dove's Significance*

The series' recurrent motif, the title Black Doves, is more than just a lyrical moniker. The darkness of betrayal and espionage is contrasted with doves, which are frequently used as symbols of purity and serenity. Subtle black doves can be seen in the background of important scenes, including a piece of jewellery Reed wears in Episode 5 and a mural in Helen's flat.

The series' main themes—the loss of innocence and the dualism of light and shadow—are brought to light via these visual cues.

2. *Hidden Names in the Background*

Astute viewers may observe that some names recur frequently in the background of scenes—on street signs, documents, and even graffiti. These characters' names frequently hint at their eventual significance and are associated with key roles in the mystery as it develops.

For example, long before Tracey Ullman's character Alex is fully introduced, a brief scene in Episode 2 depicts the name "Alex Kane" written on a wall.

3. *Historical References to London*

With subtle references to actual espionage and subterranean networks, the series honours London's past. At Episode 4, a meeting is held at an abandoned Underground station, alluding to real stations that were utilised for espionage work during the war.

To guarantee accuracy, the production team collaborated extensively with historians, giving the series' setting an additional degree of reality.

4. *The Specifics of Helen's Past*

Little clues about Helen's enigmatic history are scattered throughout the series, allowing viewers to piece together her past. A picture on her desk in Episode 3 depicts her with a number of unnamed people, one of whom is remarkably similar to a recurrent enemy.

These hints support fan ideas that Helen may have been more deeply involved in the field of espionage than first thought.

5. *Clues from Colour Palettes*

Subtle narrative clues are provided by the show's use of colour. Warmer tones emerge at intimate or vulnerable occasions, while chilly tones are frequently used around Helen, expressing her composed and aloof personality.

Remarkably, Reed regularly uses sharp black-and-white contrasts in her settings, signifying her moral ambivalence and the ongoing conflict between loyalty and treachery.

Chapter 10: The Hopes for Season 2 and Renewal

Netflix's trust in Black Doves is demonstrated by the announcement of a second season renewal, which was made months before the first season premiere. The choice to approve Season 2 is a reflection of the excitement surrounding the program as well as the excellent cast and gripping plot. The importance of the renewal, possible plot lines, and what fans are looking forward to in the upcoming installment are all covered in this chapter.

The Disclosure: Netflix's Belief in Black Doves

Given that the first season had not yet aired, Netflix made the unusual and audacious announcement that Black Doves would return for a second season in August 2024. Both fans and industry insiders were rather excited by this development, which cemented the show's place as a star in the streaming behemoth's lineup.

A number of reasons, including the well-known cast, Joe Barton's track record, and Black Doves' clever placement inside the enduringly famous spy thriller genre, probably had an impact on Netflix's decision. Black Doves' universal themes of love, devotion, and betrayal make it a prime contender for long-term success, and the streaming service has made significant investments in original programming that appeals to people throughout the world.

Additionally, its early renewal shows a dedication to long-term narrative. By announcing Season 2, Netflix gives fans the assurance that the complex storylines and unsolved mysteries that were presented in Season 1 will have time to develop further, avoiding the problems associated with shows that are discontinued too soon.

The cast and crew were thrilled to hear the announcement, with Joe Barton hinting that the second season would be *"even more ambitious, with twists no one will see coming"* and Keira Knightley calling it *"an incredible opportunity to delve deeper into Helen's story."*

Potential Storylines for Season Two

It is anticipated that Black Doves' first season would conclude with major cliffhangers and unanswered mysteries, laying the groundwork for an exciting sequel. Although exact plot points are still unknown, the following possible paths have generated conjecture:

1. *The Revealed Secret Past of Helen*
A major theme of the show is Helen's enigmatic past; Season 1 provides enticing clues but no conclusive solutions. The events that lead her to become involved in the realm of espionage could be revealed in

Season 2, which would go deeper into her past.

New characters from Helen's history may be introduced during this investigation; some may be threats, while others may be allies. Flashbacks could deepen her character development by shedding light on her reasons and setting the scene for her choices.

2. *Reed's Role and Allegiances*

One of the most mysterious characters in the series is still Reed, played by Sarah Lancashire. Her loyalties might be examined in more detail in Season 2, demonstrating if she genuinely supports Helen or has other plans. Reed's dualism offers a chance to look more closely at topics of betrayal and trust. The chemistry between her and Helen could change in surprising ways, and their relationship could take unexpected turns.

3. *Making the Underworld Bigger*

Black Doves heavily relies on London's criminal underworld, which might be expanded in Season 2 to include additional factions and power battles. As Helen and her supporters traverse an increasingly perilous terrain, these developments would increase the stakes. Jason, played by Andrew Koji, might play a bigger part as a link between Helen's espionage efforts and the criminal organisations she has to deal with.

4. *A Novel Mission with Worldwide Consequences*

Helen's personal journey is the main emphasis of Season 1, but Season 2 may expand to include a mission with more significant geopolitical ramifications. This change will not only increase the suspense but also establish Black Doves as a spy thriller series that can address global concerns.

What Fans Hope to See Up Next

Because of their intense interest in the plot and characters, Black Doves fans have already started to share their predictions and hypotheses regarding Season 2. The following are a few of the most common requests:

1. *Additional Character Development*
Characters like Jason (Andrew Koji) and Sam (Ben Whishaw), whose roles in Season 1 suggested more promise, have viewers excited to learn more about the supporting cast. In order to enhance the story, fans would like to see these characters' motivations and backstories examined in more detail. A greater emphasis on relationships, particularly the intricacies of Helen's love connections and her changing dynamic with Reed, is also demanded.

2. *More Powerful Female Storylines*
Fans hope that the show's representation of complex female characters, which has

received accolades, will continue in Season 2. Viewers want to see the stories of Helen and Reed, in particular, stay at the forefront of the espionage thriller genre since they are regarded as pioneers in the field.

To further broaden the narrative landscape, there is also interest in creating additional female characters, either as rivals or friends.

3. *More Drama with High Stakes and Action*

Fans enjoy Black Doves' exciting action scenes as much as its emotional depth. With more intricate set pieces and heated confrontations, many people are hoping that Season 2 will up the ante. Deeper examination of the psychological costs of espionage may be used to supplement these high-stakes drama moments, giving the action more depth and keeping it rooted in the narrative's themes.

4. *Solving Important Mysteries*

Fans are anxious for Season 2 to offer answers to the many questions that Season 1 is predicted to leave open. The most important of these are the secrets of Helen's history and the actual nature of Reed's allegiances. In order for the story to seem complete and fulfilling, viewers also want to see a resolution to the complex plotting and foreshadowing in Season 1.

5. *Preserving the Harmony of Intimacy and Interest*

Black Doves's ability to strike a balance between personal character moments and general intrigue is one of its defining features. Supporters are eager for this equilibrium to be maintained, with the show continuing to explore the characters' inner lives in greater detail while retaining its edge as an espionage thriller.

CONCLUSION

The Black Dove's Allure

Black Doves' powerful fusion of drama, mystery, and emotional depth has captivated both critics and viewers. Fundamentally, the series is a study of moral complexity, human resilience, and the difficulties of trust and treachery rather than merely a compelling spy thriller.

The genre is redefined by Joe Barton's vision, which is realised through an outstanding ensemble and a beautifully complex story that demonstrates that espionage stories can be both intimate and wide. Even while the program explores a dark world of secrets, its deft handling of personal issues with high-stakes risk strikes a deep chord and makes it accessible.

While its contemporary storytelling guarantees relevance in today's streaming environment, its setting, characters, and issues invoke a timeless appeal. Black Doves challenges viewers to reevaluate their preconceptions, get emotionally invested in its complex world, and develop relationships with its characters at every turn.

Future Plans for the Series and Its Fans

Black Doves promises a future as compelling as its present as Season 1 draws to a close and anticipation for Season 2 grows. Fans can anticipate more in-depth examinations of unsolved mysteries, changing relationships, and ever-higher stakes as a result of Netflix's early renewal, which shows the streaming service's dedication to pursuing the plot.

The secrets alluded to in Season 1 might be revealed in the upcoming chapter of the show, especially in regards to Helen's mysterious past and Reed's conflicting allegiances. The show might be able to examine more extensive geopolitical problems while maintaining its close-knit emphasis on character-driven storytelling if it were to broaden its narrative scope.

The journey for fans doesn't stop with the actual episodes. Black Doves will continue to be a cultural icon thanks to theories, conversations, and a mutual enthusiasm for what lies ahead. The fact that a show can elicit such enthusiastic participation and expectation is evidence of the storytelling power of the medium.

Black Doves is positioned to make a lasting impact on the spy thriller genre, whether it is by introducing new characters and twists or by extending well-loved plotlines. The series' appeal to its viewers is derived from both what it discloses and the limitless potential of what is yet to come.

One thing is evident as the narrative progresses: Black Doves is more than just a show; it's an immersive experience that captivates, challenges, and thrills audiences, leaving them eagerly anticipating the next installment of its remarkable story.

Printed in Great Britain
by Amazon